STEAMERS AT THE S

Steam Colliers of the North-East

1841-1945

*First the Dudgeon
Then the Spurn,
Flamborough Head
Comes next in turn.
Filey Brigg, that very high land
Is many miles from Sunderland.
The Old Man says if things go right
We'll be in Tyne
Tomorrow night.*

RICHARD E. KEYS · 1999

Dick Keys and Ken Smith

Tyne Bridge Publishing

Acknowledgements:

The authors wish to thank the following for their kind help in the preparation of this book: Sammy Allen, Jarrow; Bob Balmer, Blyth; Stan Bryson, Gateshead; Ian Cameron, Newcastle; Russ Campbell, Stephenson Clarke Shipping Ltd.; Jim Cuthbert, Jarrow; A. Duncan, Gravesend; Andrew Flaws, Shetland; Ron French, Wooler; Wilson Glanville, Ovington; Michael Irwin, Newcastle; Bernard Kent, Newcastle; Adrian Osler, Newcastle; Len Slater, North Shields; Newcastle Libraries & Information Service; Blyth Local Studies Group; Tyne & Wear Archives; Guildhall Library, London.

Photographs are copyright of Newcastle Libraries & Information Service unless otherwise indicated.

Published by
Tyne Bridge Publishing
City of Newcastle upon Tyne
Education & Libraries Directorate
Newcastle Libraries & Information Service
2000

ISBN: 1 85795 160 3

British Library Cataloguing in Publication data: a catalogue record for this book is available from the British Library.

Printed by Bailes the Printer, Houghton le Spring

Front cover: *Returning for coal. A France, Fenwick collier approaches the open Swing Bridge between Newcastle and Gateshead in the early 1900s, probably on her way to Dunston Staiths to load coal.*

Back cover: *Trimmers at Blyth in the early 1900s. (Blyth Local Studies Group)*

Other Maritime History books from Newcastle Libraries & Information Service:

By Dick Keys and Ken Smith:
Black Diamonds by Sea: North-East Sailing Colliers 1780-1880, £5.99
Down Elswick Slipways: Armstrong's Ships & People 1884-1918, £5.99
From Walker to the World: Charles Mitchell's Low Walker Shipyard, £4.99

By Ken Smith:
Mauretania: Pride of the Tyne, £4.99
Turbinia: The Story of Charles Parsons and his Ocean Greyhound, £4.99
Tyne to Titanic: The Story of Rescue Ship Carpathia, £4.99

By Ian Rae and Ken Smith:
Built with Pride: Tyne Ships 1969-1994, £4.99

Catalogue available from:

Tyne Bridge Publishing
Newcastle Libraries & Information Service
City Library
Princess Square
Newcastle upon Tyne
NE99 1DX

www.newcastle.gov.uk/tynebridgepublishing

Contents

Illustrations

SWING BRIDGE & QUAYSIDE, NEWCASTLE-ON-TYNE.

Returning for coal. A France, Fenwick collier approaches the open Swing Bridge between Newcastle and Gateshead in the early 1900s, probably on her way to Dunston Staiths to load coal. People can be seen waiting on the Newcastle side of the bridge for the ship to pass.

~Early Wonders~

In March 1841 an iron-hulled propeller-driven steamship was launched into the River Tyne in North-East England at the South Shields shipyard of Thomas Marshall. Those witnessing the birth of the steamer *Bedlington* could not have realised that this small vessel heralded a revolution in the delivery of coal by sea from the pits of Northumberland and County Durham.

This revolution would lead to the gradual decline of the old sailing collier ships which for centuries had delivered the black diamonds of the North-East to London and other ports in Britain and Europe. Sail would be replaced by steam as the motive force for this flourishing seaborne trade. A steamship could ensure fast, regular deliveries of coal and was not dependent on the vagaries of the wind which might hold up a sailing collier for many days or drive her on to the shore or sandbanks of the East Coast.

The *Bedlington* was in many ways an extraordinary ship for her time. She was built for the Bedlington Coal Company to carry waggons of coal from the River Blyth to the mouth of the Tyne. Rails were laid in her large hold to take the waggons and the vessel was equipped with a steam derrick to lift them aboard.

When the *Bedlington* had reached Shields Harbour the steam derrick's task was to lift the waggons aboard waiting sailing colliers, placing them over the holds of the ships for the coal to be loaded by opening doors in the bottoms of the waggons.

Another novel feature of the vessel was her water ballast tanks which did away with the need to carry solid ballast. In addition, unusually at that date, she was equipped with two propellers. Her engines were situated at the stern and the boilers were placed in the fore part of the ship, with the connecting pipes running along the sides of the vessel.

However, almost from the start the *Bedlington* was beset with problems and frequent repairs were needed. In February 1846 she ran aground on a sandbank in the River Blyth and was badly damaged. She was eventually repaired but in 1850 the coal company

Artist's impression by Dick Keys

The steam collier Bedlington, *completed in 1841, at Shields Harbour. She carried coal from the River Blyth to the mouth of the Tyne, where it was loaded on to sailing ships. Her boilers were in the fore part of the ship.*

managed to establish a rail link with the Tyne. The *Bedlington* was no longer needed and the following year the ship was sold to owners at Leith on the Firth of Forth.

The vessel, which was the first iron-hulled propeller-driven steam collier in the world, was requisitioned for service during the Crimean War and suffered the fate of being sunk by Russian shore batteries in 1854.

The *Bedlington* had been a daring experiment. But the ingenuity of North-East shipbuilders, engineers and inventors was not to be dimmed. In July 1844 another propeller-driven steamship, which carried sails, was launched on the Tyne, this time from the yard of John Coutts at Low Walker, Newcastle.

Named the *Q.E.D.*, she was rigged as a barque and fitted with two steam reciprocating engines. The 150ft-long ship was also fitted with watertight bulkheads and double bottom plating which as well as providing extra protection also formed water ballast tanks. These two features alone put the *Q.E.D.*, like the *Bedlington*, in the vanguard of shipbuilding. In common with many early steamships her sails were intended to be used when winds were favourable to

conserve fuel. The engines were operated mainly in head winds or calms.

In September 1844 she left the Tyne on her maiden voyage to London with a cargo of coal, but during the trip ran aground on the Gunfleet Sand off Clacton, Essex. A small part of the cargo had to be jettisoned to lighten her and she eventually floated free. Arriving in the Thames, she moored off the Princess Stairs, Rotherhithe, and attracted a great deal of attention.

But the *Q.E.D.* soon began carrying general cargoes as well as coal. In April 1845 she was advertised as 'loading for Montreal direct'. She left the Tyne for Canada on May 2 with a varied cargo. The ship was carrying 25,542 glass window panes, two portrait paintings with gilt frames, 12 pairs of stockings, 45 chaldrons of coal and 148 tons of cinders. Stopping at Plymouth ten days later, she reached Montreal after a 48-day passage from the Tyne, a by no means fast time, even in those days.

Later in her career the *Q.E.D.*'s engines were removed and she became purely a sailing vessel. She was wrecked near Le Havre in 1855 while bound from the Tyne to Rouen with black diamonds.

In October 1845 another early steamer was completed in the North-East. Appropriately named the *Experiment*, she was built by coal owner John Ray on the River Wear at Sunderland. Schooner-rigged, she was equipped with 80hp engines and had a wooden hull. However, it is clear the *Experiment* was not intended solely for the coal trade and carried general cargo as well as passengers on a service operating from Sunderland to London. Later it would be mistakenly claimed that she was the first regular steam collier.

The *Experiment*'s career did not last long. She stayed on the Sunderland-London goods and passenger trade throughout 1846, but caught fire while anchored off the Essex coast in April the following year. A revenue cutter took her in tow but she was ablaze from stem to stern and eventually sank.

However, these three vessels were merely forerunners of a much more significant ship, the *John Bowes*. She was to cause the greatest stir in the North-East.

Dick Keys

The Q.E.D, *which was built at the yard of John Coutts, Low Walker.*

~The Pioneer~

The iron-hulled propeller-driven *John Bowes* is generally regarded as the most important pioneering steamship to carry coal. The Tyne-built vessel certainly made a much greater impact than her predecessors when she entered service in 1852. She demonstrated that a steamship could deliver her cargo to its destination with a speed and regularity which a sailing collier could not hope to match. In addition, the *John Bowes* was the first steamer built specifically for the black diamonds trade between the North-East and London.

She was launched at the Jarrow shipyard of Palmer Brothers on June 30 1852. The naming ceremony was performed by the wife of Charles Palmer, the Tyneside businessman whose ideas had led to the building of the vessel.

Ironically, the ship's birth had been prompted by competition from land transport. The development of railways led to the fast delivery of coal to London and the South East from the mines of the northern Midlands and Yorkshire. Steam trains delivered 8,000 tons of coal to the capital in 1845. The amounts then began to increase dramatically. In 1851 the figure had reached 248,000 tons.

Mine owners in the North-East were worried by this challenge. There was even talk of delivering coal by rail from the Tyne to London. But Charles Palmer, who had been born at South Shields and had shares in collieries, believed the challenge from steam on the land could be met by the use of steam on the sea. Charles became one of the directors of the newly-formed General Iron Screw Collier Company, which he and other businessmen had formed to operate steamships on the East Coast coal runs.

The *Newcastle Journal* commented a few days after the launch of the *John Bowes* in 1852 that: 'for 600 years have the denizens of the coaly Tyne been content to transport the black diamonds to various parts of the world in the old fashioned collier, and the lapse of time has scarcely witnessed any improvement in their construction. The immense opposition given to sea transport by the establishment of the railways caused Palmer Brothers & Co to build the *John Bowes*'.

Dick Keys

The John Bowes, *launched at Jarrow in 1852. She was the first vessel to clearly demonstrate the advantages of delivering coal by steamship. Her long career lasted 81 years, during which she suffered many collisions and mishaps.*

Charles Palmer had founded his shipyard at Jarrow with his brother, George, a year earlier and the new collier was only the second vessel built there. However, within a few years the construction of steam colliers was to become one of the mainstays of the yard.

The launch of the ship certainly stirred up great interest on Tyneside. Charles Palmer was more than happy to attract publicity for the venture. Coal owners and manufacturers were among the large number of people who attended. Guests included the Mayor and Sheriff of Newcastle. At 2.15 in the afternoon, which was high tide, the ship, nearly 150ft long, glided into the Tyne without any major problem.

Afterwards, 300 guests attended a dinner at the yard, followed by a ball in the evening. Charles and the Mayor's wife led off the

Charles Mark Palmer, the man behind the building of the pioneering steam collier John Bowes, *the first steam ship built specifically to operate on the black diamonds run between the North-East and London.*

dancing. Hopes in the success of the *John Bowes* must have been high.

Those hopes were to be fulfilled in great measure. The ship left the Tyne on her maiden voyage with a cargo of coal on July 27 1852, under the command of a Captain John Scott. She halted at Sunderland for compass adjustment. From there, it took her two days to reach London, two days to discharge her cargo in the Thames and she was back in the Tyne on August 3. The round voyage had taken her only seven days, as against a sailing collier's usual month. She had carried 500 tons of coal, although she was capable of taking up to 650 tons.

The fast voyage had been achieved even though the *John Bowes* had been 'running in' her new engines by operating them at little more than half speed. Her two single-cylinder engines had been built by the renowned firm of Robert Stephenson at Forth Banks, Newcastle. This machinery gave her a top speed of about eight or nine knots. Later in the ship's career she was fitted with new, improved engines, although like most early seagoing steamers she also carried sails, being rigged as a topsail schooner.

Palmer's yard at Jarrow went on to build many more steam colliers. It was not long before the speed and coal-carrying achievements of the *John Bowes* had been surpassed by some of these new vessels. During the year 1854 the Palmer-built collier *Jarrow* made 29 voyages to London, delivering a total of 18,006 tons.

In 1859 the yard built the *James Dixon*. She could carry 1,200 tons of black diamonds and made the voyage from the North-East to London and back in three days, four hours. The *James Dixon* made 57 voyages to London in one year, delivering a total of 62,842 tons of coal with a crew of 22 men. To accomplish this work with sailing colliers would have required 16 ships and 144 men.

The pioneering *John Bowes* had a long career lasting 81 years, during which she carried general cargo as well as coal. In 1854 she was brought into service, along with other Palmer-built steam colliers, to carry stores to troops in the Crimean War. The ship also changed ownership several times.

Her career had more than its fair share of accidents and

mishaps. Indeed, she seems to have been bedevilled by a series of collisions. For example, on December 31 1856 she was in collision with the *Helen Day*, of Dundee, when off Souter Point, to the north of Sunderland. The *John Bowes* received considerable damage, including the loss of her mizzen mast.

In September 1858 she collided with the schooner *Tweed*, owned by the Berwick Shipping Company, at 1am one morning when six miles south of Orfordness, Suffolk. The *Tweed* was badly damaged and lost one man overboard.

In April the following year came a more unusual accident. The *Newcastle Courant* reported that 'while discharging an immense iron target, one of the *John Bowes*' runner blocks carried away and the target swung on board again, carrying away the funnel which came into contact with the main mast, knocking it over the stern. Three dockyard labourers were slightly injured'.

In 1864, while on a voyage from the Tyne to Hamburg, she ran aground on rocks near the island of Heligoland, about 15 miles from the entrance to the River Elbe. Part of her cargo was thrown overboard in an effort to lighten the ship. She eventually floated free but was beached in a sinking state. The leak was then patched up and she continued on her voyage to Hamburg.

The next year the *John Bowes* was involved in two more collisions. In September she was in collision with a sailing vessel called the *Aimwell*, 10 miles north of Seaham. The *Aimwell* was badly damaged. December saw her run into the brig *Albion*, which was moored at North Shields. The steamer had been entering the river.

The year 1868 witnessed yet another collision. At 1am she collided with the steamer *Sappho* in the mouth of the Tyne. The *John Bowes* was inward bound at the time of the accident.

The next mishap occurred in November 1884 at 3am. She was moving up the Thames near the West India Dock when she collided with the iron steamer *Blanche*, outward bound for Dunkirk. The *Blanche* sank, although it is not recorded whether there was any loss of life.

In early September 1888 it was the turn of the *John Bowes* to receive damage. While leaving the Tyne for London, her steering gear failed and she hit the South Pier, suffering serious damage to her stem. Her fore compartment filled with water. A tug took her to Jarrow Slake where she lay forlornly on the mud.

She was repaired and put back in service. Her history of collisions was, however, far from over. In December 1890 she was in collision with the steamer *Braemar*, from Aberdeen, off Whitehill Point in the Tyne.

The year 1898 saw her in a Thames collision with the steamer *Eslington*, managed by the firm of W. Runciman, Newcastle. The *Eslington* had been built at Wallsend in 1876. Both ships were coal laden. The bow of the *John Bowes* was damaged and the *Eslington* had to be beached near the Victoria Dock. The *Eslington* was later repaired and refloated, surviving until 1903 when she went missing in the North Sea.

The pioneering Palmer collier's long accident record continued. In June 1898, only a few months after the Thames collision, she got into difficulties while on passage from Glasgow to Waterford. She put into Strangford Lough in Northern Ireland, but on coming out, struck a reef. However, she eventually floated off.

The catalogue of mishaps went on. Next came a collision off the Lancashire coast with the Crosby Lightship, which was badly damaged. Afterwards, she was in collision, again in the Thames, with a collier and received severe damage. The *John Bowes* was arrested by the Admiralty Marshall. After being released, she was sold to Norwegian owners and renamed *Spec*. During her time under this ownership her master committed suicide while the ship was moored in Shields Harbour.

Later came other changes of name and ownership. Eventually, after a long and useful, but accident-packed life, she came to grief in 1933 off the coast of northern Spain, while sailing under the name of *Villa Selgas* for Spanish owners. The old ship sank after developing a leak in rough seas. She was carrying a cargo of iron ore. All the crew were saved.

By a strange irony, 1933 was also the year in which the Palmer shipbuilding business at Jarrow finally collapsed, leading to mass unemployment in the town.

~Tyne Coal~

The development of steam colliers helped to generate a great increase in coal shipments from the rivers of the North-East. One of the most important markets was the emerging gas industry of London which needed a plentiful and regular supply of black diamonds to produce gas lighting for the capital's streets. In the 20th century, the power stations of the electricity industry would also provide vital work for the colliers.

Before 1850 coal exports from the River Tyne had grown to about five and a quarter million tons a year, but between then and the early 1900s the shipments increased enormously. In 1911 more

A ship loading coal at a Tyne staith in 1897. Trimmers can be seen on the right. Note the spout or chute down which the coal cascaded into the hold.

than 20 million tons of coal and coke were exported from the river to London, the South-East and other ports throughout Britain and the world. In 1913 exports again reached over 20 million tons. Although this figure fell during the First World War, shipments recovered afterwards, reaching more than 21 million tons in 1923.

This booming seaborne trade was greatly assisted by the establishment in 1850 of the Tyne Improvement Commission which made the river one of the best ports on the East Coast. Beginning in the 1860s, the commission carried out major dredging operations which deepened the Tyne and enabled it to take larger ships as well as improving life for the smaller ones.

The treacherous bar at the mouth of the river was dredged away and the Tyne, for a distance of 14 miles inland from the mouth, was widened and straightened. Islands in the waterway were dredged away. Bill Point at Walker and Whitehill Point at North Shields, protruding sections of the shore which were a hazard to navigation, were removed.

The Tyne's impressive protective North and South Piers were constructed at the river mouth. Work began on the North Pier in 1854 but it was beset with problems, being breached by storms in 1867 and again, more seriously, in 1897. The structure was therefore redesigned so that it would be straight, rather than curved. The pier was finally completed in 1909 and opened to the public the following year. The longer South Pier was begun in 1854 and finished in 1895.

The commission also improved facilities for the loading of coal so that steamers could take on their cargoes quickly and efficiently. The Tyne gained a well deserved reputation as a port for bunkering. Ships seeking coal to refuel their engines could speedily and cheaply replenish their bunkers at staiths (loading jetties) not far

Faces of character. Trimmers at Blyth in the early 1900s. Trimmers, armed with shovels levelled out the coal in the holds, helping to ensure stability and enabling the hatches to be closed. They worked in tandem with teemers, who carried out the actual loading of vessels, operating the equipment needed for this process.

The entrance to Northumberland Dock, which was opened in 1857. It contained eight staiths, four operated by Northumberland coal companies and four by the London and North Eastern Railway.

witnessed the increasing introduction of electric conveyor belts, an important advance which improved the efficiency of loading, particularly at high tides.

By 1925 there were six major coal loading points on the Tyne. They were: Tyne Dock, Dunston Staiths, and West Dunston Staiths, owned by the London and North Eastern Railway (formerly the North Eastern Railway); Northumberland Dock and Whitehill Point Staiths, owned by the Tyne Improvement Commission; and Derwenthaugh Staiths, owned by the Consett Iron Company. All were equipped with gravity spouts and electric conveyor belts. Staiths were also provided by the Tyne Improvement Commission at the Albert Edward Dock, North Shields.

In addition, there were a considerable number of smaller staiths, often owned by colliery companies, such as Harton Staiths at South Shields and those at Wallsend, Hebburn, Felling, and Elswick.

One of the most important loading facilities was at Tyne Dock on the south bank, which by 1925 had exported more coal than any other dock in the world. In 1908, 7.5 million tons of coal and coke had cascaded from its staiths into the holds of waiting ships. The dock had four staiths, which enabled 16 vessels to load at the same time. There were 42 spouts and eight electric conveyor belts. Two or more spouts could be operated on one steamer simultaneously, thus achieving rapid loading.

The London and North Eastern Railway declared in an advertisement of 1925: 'Tyne Dock has the reputation for giving the quickest despatch in the country to vessels taking coal. Situated near the mouth of the River Tyne, the dock offers exceptional facilities for quick bunkering.'

At Northumberland Dock, Howdon, on the north side of the river, which was opened in 1857, there were eight staiths, four operated by coal companies of South-East Northumberland and four by

from the river mouth and so achieve a quick turn-around time at low cost.

The ships were attended to by shore-based workmen known as teemers and trimmers. The teemers carried out the actual loading of vessels, operating the equipment needed for this process. The trimmers, armed with shovels, would level out the coal in the holds, helping to ensure stability and enabling the hatches to be closed by 'knocking the top off' the black diamonds.

One of the earliest loading methods was the waggon drop, a system in which a coal truck was lowered from the staith on to the deck of a ship. A door was then opened in the bottom of the waggon and the coal would cascade into the hold. Alternatively, a waggon would remain on a staith, the doors in its bottom would be opened and the cargo allowed to stream down a spout (also known as a chute) into the ship. This gravity spout method eventually superseded the waggon drop, becoming the most common arrangement on the North-East coast. The early years of the 20th century the London and North Eastern Railway.

Also on the north side, on a bend in the river a little to the east of Northumberland Dock, were the Whitehill Point Staiths. These were often used by bunkering ships which did not have time to enter the dock and which could be replenished with coal at any state of the tide. However, the staiths also loaded colliers with their cargo. The facility featured three hydraulic lifts which could raise trucks up to 45ft above the jetties, allowing large ships to be coaled by electric conveyor belts no matter how high the tide. Ten miles up river, beyond the great bridges across the Tyne between Newcastle and Gateshead, lay the important Dunston Staiths, opened in 1893. These were built to handle the output of coal from pits west of central Newcastle and Gateshead to save the time and cost taken by the longer rail journey to the docks nearer the river mouth. A second set of staiths was added to the facility in 1903.

At Dunston, the loading of ships from the six berths could also be undertaken at any state of the tide, a tribute to the dredging work of the Tyne Improvement Commission. Each berth had two gravity spouts and there were three conveyor belts.

Colliers steamed up river to Dunston, moving through the open Swing Bridge as crowds of walkers on the Newcastle and Gateshead sides waited patiently for them to pass. When close to the staiths they would generally moor at lines of buoys (tiers), joining a queue of vessels waiting for their turn to load.

In 1923 West Dunston Staiths were opened, over a mile to the west, expanding the facilities to meet increased demand. Furthest west of the major coal jetties were the Derwenthaugh Staiths. These were situated a little to the east of the Scotswood Bridge on the southern bank close to the mouth of the Derwent.

The facilities at Dunston, West Dunston and Derwenthaugh, between 10 and 11 miles from the sea, had been made possible by

Frank & Son, Gateshead

A view of Dunston Staiths in the early 1920s, with a collier alongside. The ship is the Lolin, *of San Sebastian, Spain, an indication that many foreign vessels visited the Tyne to load coal. The* Lolin *had been completed in 1897 at West Hartlepool by Furness Withy as the* Annie, *her first owners being British. The tug on the left is probably the* Oscar, *built in 1876 and owned by Joseph Ridley of South Shields. A locomotive can be seen on the staith.*

the commission's dredging work and by the removal of Newcastle's 18th century bridge of low arches and its replacement with the Swing Bridge, completed in 1876.

The year 1924 saw 6,007 ships pass through the Swing Bridge, the majority of them colliers. As a ship approached the bridge, from either direction, she sounded three blasts on her steam whistle. The bridge then answered this signal with three blasts from its own siren and the opening machinery was started.

In the 1930s two new staiths were opened at Howdon and Jarrow, featuring electric conveyor belts which delivered the coal to special towers from which it was loaded into the waiting ships. The Howdon staith, at the western end of Northumberland Dock, was

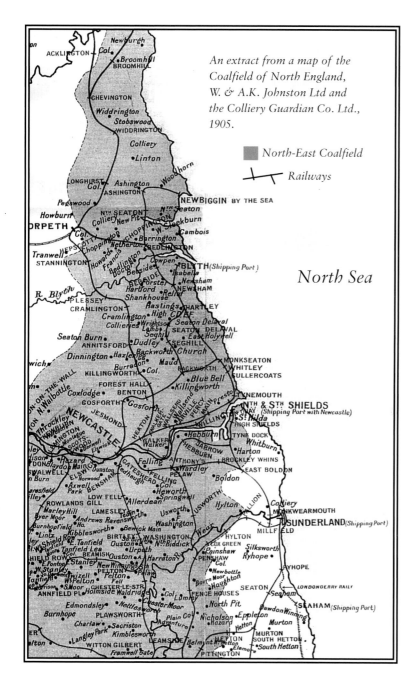

An extract from a map of the Coalfield of North England, W. & A.K. Johnston Ltd and the Colliery Guardian Co. Ltd., 1905.

North-East Coalfield

Railways

North Sea

opened in December 1932 by the chairman of the Tyne Improvement Commission, Harry P. Everett. Visiting a sub-station, he switched on the electric current, enabling coal to be loaded into the colliers *Dagenham* and *Corbrook*. The Jarrow facility began operating in 1936.

However, the mundane staiths of the Tyne were not without their moments of drama. Most were constructed of timber, making them a major fire risk.

At about 10pm on March 3 1905 a fierce blaze broke out at Cramlington No 5 Staith at Whitehill Point. It was believed that an axle on a coal truck had become overheated and had set fire to the truck. Whatever the cause, the flames quickly spread to the wooden staith which was saturated in tar and covered in coal dust.

The North Shields and dock fire brigades were quickly on the scene but the fire had spread rapidly and they arrived to find the 500-ft long staith engulfed in flames. The glare lit up the sky and could be seen for miles around. The firemen were unable to get within 50ft of the staith because of the intense heat.

With difficulty, an engine managed to haul a line of blazing trucks off the staith. The fire then spread to a timber shed which was burnt to the ground. At about midnight the entire staith collapsed, sending up a shower of sparks which fell on to pit props lying nearby. These too were set ablaze.

The Cape liner *Johannesburg*, which had been taking on bunker coal, was towed away from the staith on fire amidships. She was said to have been lucky to escape destruction.

The blaze was not put out until 14 hours after it began. The German steamer *Mongolia*, arriving in the Tyne early on March 4, reported that the glare of the inferno had been seen four miles off the coast.

Luckily, there had been no loss of life or injuries. Tools owned by the staith's workmen were destroyed when the timber shed in which they were stored was burnt down. The Tyne Improvement Commissioners agreed to compensate them for their loss. Cramlington No 5 Staith was eventually rebuilt.

~Ships and Crews~

A steam collier was a vessel specialising mainly in the transport of black diamonds, often engaged on the runs to London, the South Coast, or near Continental ports.

However, many general cargo ships, some operating for Tyne-based owners, would leave the river with holds full of coal. This was, understandably, the commonest outward cargo. They would return to the Tyne with a wide variety of goods and materials. Timber from the Baltic for pit props and railway sleepers was a favourite inward item.

In addition, a large number of foreign ships visited the Tyne and the Wear to collect coal for which Northumberland and Durham was renowned worldwide.

Many of the crewmen on the runs from the Tyne to the South were Geordies. The men of South Shields in particular had a long seafaring tradition and few colliers from the river were without some men from this well-placed seaside town. Other areas of Tyneside were also well represented among the crews, with sometimes a sprinkling of Scots and Cockneys.

The colliers operated a watch-ashore, watch-aboard system of working for deck crews which enabled the North-East men to spend time with their families while the ship was loading at their home port.

The watch-ashore men would disembark as the vessel prepared to receive her dusty cargo alongside a Tyne or Wear staith. Any delays in loading would give them more time at home. This might happen if for any reason the flow of coal by rail to the staiths was delayed or if the colliers had to stay a long time in the queues of moored ships waiting to berth.

The watch-aboard men, perhaps from London or elsewhere, would remain on board to look after the vessel and see that it was moved back and forth under the spouts as necessary. In London it would be their turn to be the watch-ashore.

However, things did not always work out this way. In practice, North-East men sometimes found themselves assigned to the watch aboard when they were in the Tyne or Wear, particularly on vessels where there were few men from other areas – a frequent occurrence. Often a man who was officially 'aboard' would go ashore by

A ship is loaded at Dunston Staiths around 1920. Coal piles up on the fore-deck. A spout or chute is seen on the left.

The Jetblack, *built in 1920 and owned by the Gas Light and Coke Company. An old-style engines amidships collier, like the* Gaslight *below, she completed well over 1,000 voyages in a career lasting 34 years.*

Long career. The Gaslight *was completed by Wood Skinner of Bill Quay, Gateshead, in 1920. Owned by the Gas Light and Coke Company, she survived an aircraft attack during the Second World War and was not broken up until 1957.*

arrangement with his mates, who stayed behind to look after the ship. When he came back another man would have a turn ashore.

The ships these men sailed in were unglamorous but sturdy little one-funnel steamers with wide hold openings, which voyaged back and forth from the North-East to southern England and near Continental ports, with their commonplace but vital cargo. Many of the vessels were built at shipyards on the Tyne and at Sunderland and Blyth. Their engines too were often supplied by North-East companies.

Both engines and bridge were sited amidships in the majority of steam colliers during the first 60 years or so of the steam era, although in many of the early Palmer colliers they had been placed aft. However, the 20th century saw an engines aft, bridge amidships layout gain increasing favour. Colliers with their engines amidships became the 'old timers'.

Propelling machinery was gradually improved over the years. The triple expansion engine was adopted by most coal-carrying steam ships in the 20th century. After the Second World War steam suffered a decline and diesel motor engines were increasingly used to drive vessels.

A round voyage in peacetime from the Tyne to London and back might take anything from three to six days, depending on how long a ship had to wait at the buoys to discharge and whether strong north-easterly head winds were encountered on the run home in ballast. When gales blew from this direction, as they frequently did, the colliers might drop their anchors and shelter behind Flamborough Head or in Yarmouth Roads, waiting for the wind to drop. Fog could also cause considerable delays.

By the 1890s it was common for a collier in the Tyne to load a 1,000 ton cargo in four to five hours and then make the voyage to London and back in four days.

Iron ships lasted longer than those constructed of steel. As we have seen, the iron-hulled *John Bowes* lasted 81 years. In the 20th century, if a steel steam collier managed to survive war and the perils of the elements she might have a life of 30 years or more, completing well over 1,000 voyages.

For example, the Gas Light and Coke Company's *Jetblack*, launched in 1920, had a career lasting nearly 34 years. She came through the Second World War unscathed and by 1949 had notched up over 1,200 voyages. The ship survived until 1954 when she was broken up at Dunston.

Another long-lived ship was the *Gaslight*, which was completed by Wood Skinner of Bill Quay, Gateshead, in 1920. Although damaged by aircraft attack in 1941, she was repaired at Sunderland and went back into service for the Gas Light & Coke Company of London. The *Gaslight* was eventually sold to new owners but was not broken up until 1957.

Some of the most important of the many shipping companies to operate steam colliers on the East Coast runs were Stephenson Clarke; William Cory & Sons; William France, Fenwick; the Hudson Steam Ship Company; the Constantine Steam Ship Company, and W.A. Souter and its associated business, the Sheaf Company.

One of the largest of these enterprises was Stephenson Clarke, which although based in London, had its distant origins in the North-East when two brothers, Ralph and Robert Clarke, of Longbenton and later North Shields, set up a shipowning business

The North and South Piers made the entry to the Tyne safer for shipping. The South Pier, from which this picture was taken, was completed in 1895 but the North Pier suffered storm damage and was not finally completed until 1909. This photograph dates from the early 1900s.

in the 1730s. The brothers commanded some of their own early ships.

The name Stephenson Clarke & Company was first registered in 1850 and the company developed its seaborne business with great success throughout the rest of the 19th century and into the 20th. The funnels of its vessels were painted in black with a broad silver band, earning its fleet the nickname 'silver banders'.

As well as owning ships, Stephenson Clarke took a major step forward in 1912 when it was given the management of a new, large collier, the *Fulgens*, the first vessel to be owned by the Gas Light and Coke Company. Previously, the company had chartered vessels from Stephenson Clarke and other firms.

The new ship featured an engines-aft, bridge amidships design and was equipped with a triple expansion engine built by John Dickinson of Sunderland. The *Fulgens*, which could carry almost 3,700 tons of cargo, had been built at the yard of Wood, Skinner of Bill Quay, a firm of Tyne shipbuilders which launched many steam colliers.

The ship carried coal from the North-East to the large Beckton

Andrew Flaus

Collier men. The First Mate and Steward of the collier Ferranti, *which was completed in 1932 and owned by the London Power Company. Surviving the Second World War, the* Ferranti *was broken up in 1956.*

Gas Works on the lower Thames at East Ham. Beckton was a constant hive of activity, with ships discharging 24 hours a day. Here two vessels could berth at the same time, while others waited at the buoys for their turn to go alongside.

By 1937 Stephenson Clarke was managing an entire fleet of colliers for the Gas Light and Coke Company and also for the large electricity concerns of the London Power Company, Fulham Borough Council, and Brighton Corporation. This involved deliveries of coal to destinations including Battersea, Fulham and Shoreham power stations.

Deliveries to works far up the Thames, such as those at Battersea, Fulham and Wandsworth, were made by specially designed colliers known as 'flat-irons' or 'flatties'. These up-river ships had very low superstructures with hinged funnels and hinged or telescopic masts which could be lowered, enabling them to pass under the numerous bridges. They also featured a shallow draft to combat the danger of grounding.

The first flat-irons had appeared as early as 1878, when Palmer's of Jarrow completed the *Westminster* and *Vauxhall*, designed to deliver coal from the North-East to the Nine Elms Gas Works at Vauxhall.

But the regular supply of this important cargo to the South was not achieved without a great number of tragic losses. The 18th century Tyneside brothers Ralph and Robert Clarke, forbears of the Stephenson Clarke family, were laid to rest in the cemetery on the headland at Tynemouth Priory overlooking the North Sea. That sea, a busy highway for the trade in black diamonds, was to claim the lives of many steam collier crewmen and their ships.

~Sinkings and Mysteries~

On March 12 1853 a new steam collier was launched at Palmer's Jarrow shipyard. Named the *Countess of Strathmore*, she was another early vessel of her type from the pioneering company. But her career was to be tragically short-lived.

At 8pm on July 13 of that year the *Countess of Strathmore* left Shields Harbour with a full cargo of coal, bound for London. Aboard were 15 crew and three passengers. At about midnight, the coastal waters were hit by a fierce gale. The ship ploughed bravely on southward with heavy seas breaking over her bows. It was not long before her decks were awash.

Then water began to get below decks. At noon the next day the water put her engine fires out and the pumps became choked, adding to the ship's mounting problems. She was now in great danger of sinking. The captain knew that the ship would have to make for the safety of a harbour to avoid disaster. He chose Hartlepool, and the order was given to bear away towards that port.

But worse was to come. At about 3pm an immense sea struck her which broke her wheel. The *Countess of Strathmore* had become unmanageable. The bulwarks were carried away. The position of the crew and passengers was now dire.

However, another ship, the sailing brig *Broughton*, commanded by a Captain Grey, of Boston, Lincs, sighted the steamer and realised she was in major difficulties. He managed to bring his ship close enough to attempt a rescue. By means of a rope 12 men were saved. Three more were saved by another ship which hove in sight, the *Bounty*, of Whitby, making a total of 15 survivors, including all three passengers.

The mate, William Harrison, tied himself to a ladder using the rope and was drawn through the waves towards the *Broughton*. However, tragedy struck when the heavy seas crashed against the ladder, knocking him away and he was drowned.

Captain Nicholson, the master of the *Countess of Strathmore*

Dick Keys

Tragic ship. An artist's impression of the early steam collier Countess of Strathmore, *which sank in a gale off Whitby in 1853. She had been built by Palmer's of Jarrow. The ship's captain was among three men who lost their lives. He was one of four brothers all drowned at sea.*

Violent waves pound Tynemouth pier in the late 1890s. The breach in the curve of the pier, caused by a storm, can clearly be seen. The pier was eventually rebuilt without a curve and completed in 1909.

Journal read: 'The deceased had reduced himself by his goodness of heart from affluence to be obliged to go to sea again as commander of the screw collier *Countess of Strathmore*, which vessel unfortunately foundered in the terrific gale of the 14th … when he and two crew members perished. His memory will long be cherished in his native town (North Shields) for his gentlemanly conduct and manly bearing. He was the last of four brothers who all perished in the mighty deep.'

But the *Countess of Strathmore* was not the only early collier built by Palmers to be wrecked in the North Sea. The *William Hutt,* launched in December 1852 and the second of the yard's coal steamers, came to grief off Lowestoft in late 1864. She sank with the loss of all her crew, except one man, William King, who was picked up by the fishing smack *Telegraph,* commanded by a Captain Partridge. The *William Hutt* had been trading between Sunderland and London.

Sometimes the fate of steam colliers was unknown. They simply disappeared. For example, the *Whitley Park* sailed from the Tyne in August 1856 bound for Le Havre with coal. Over a fortnight later she had failed to arrive at the French port. She and her crew were never seen again. It was reported that shortly after the *Whitley Park* left the river vessels off the East Coast encountered heavy seas. Speculation mounted that she had gone down in the Boston Deeps. The crew numbered 15 or 16. The ship had been launched at Palmer's Jarrow yard in December 1854.

Palmer-built steam colliers were, of course, by no means the only ones to disappear without trace. The *Tabor,* launched by Short Brothers at their Pallion yard, Sunderland, in June 1871, for Wearside shipowner James Westoll, was reported missing in late October 1881.

The steamer left the Tyne earlier that month with a cargo of coal for London. She had been under the command of a Captain

was the last to leave his ship. He lashed himself to a new rope. Crewmen on the brig had almost dragged him to safety when the rope broke and he fell under their stern. He too was lost. Another seaman also died when a rope parted.

The steamer sank about half an hour after the rescue, seven miles off Whitby. William Harrison, the mate, had been making his first voyage in the ship. He had been taken on the day she left the Tyne.

Captain Nicholson was the son of John Nicholson, a North Shields shipowner. The captain's three brothers had also been drowned at sea a number of years before and his parents had understandably discouraged him from taking up the sea as a career. But he had eventually become captain of the brig *Orient* and later the new steam collier.

An obituary notice on July 23 1853 in the *Newcastle Daily*

Renney. The *Tabor* was last sighted by the steamer *Hawthorns* during the height of a fierce gale off the Dudgeon. The *Hawthorns* made it safely into the Tyne but the missing collier was presumed to have sunk with the loss of all her 17 crew. Most of them were from Tyneside.

Less than two years later, in March 1883, another steam collier owned by James Westoll disappeared. She was the *Fervent*, which had also been built by Short Brothers of Sunderland. The vessel went missing after leaving the Tyne, like the ill-fated *Tabor*, bound for London with coal.

The year 1894 saw the steamer *Thurso* suffer a similar fate. In early February she sailed from the Tyne with 1,200 tons of coal bound for Hamburg. She was under the command of a Captain Hollingshead, of South Shields, and had a crew of 14. It was her first voyage for Tyne owners Thompson, Elliott of the Quayside, Newcastle.

Soon after the *Thurso*'s departure from the river a strong westerly gale developed, with winds gusting up to 60mph, which lasted for 48 hours. She failed to arrive in Hamburg. The ship had originally been named the *Eastella* and was built at Sunderland by J. Blumer in 1871.

Sometimes it seemed that ships were simply ill-fated. Three steam colliers named the *Birtley* all came to grief off the East Coast, all were built by Wood Skinner at Bill Quay, and all were owned by the Burnett Steamship Company of Newcastle.

The first *Birtley*, completed in 1900, ran ashore in fog one mile

Colliers at Dunston Staiths, around the early 1900s. The ship nearest the picture on the right is the James Westoll, *of Sunderland. The vessel was named after a leading Wearside shipowner. These staiths were owned by the London and North Eastern Railway Company.*

north of Flamborough Head on November 10 1905. She became a total wreck. The ship had been on passage from the Tyne to London with coal.

The second *Birtley*, completed in 1906, was a casualty of the First World War. She was on her way from Dunkirk to the Tyne in ballast when she was sunk by the German submarine *UB-38* in early January 1918 eight miles north of Flamborough Head. All her crew of 18 were lost.

The third ship of the name was completed at Bill Quay in 1923. She was sunk during the Second World War. The collier was bound from London to the Tyne in ballast when she hit a German mine off Cromer in September 1941. Three crewmen were killed by the explosion and the rest abandoned ship as she sank.

The name *Birtley* appears to have been distinctly unlucky.

~Black Diamonds for Hamburg~

The Tyne was the most important coal port on the North-East coast, shipping more black diamonds than any other, but it was not the only one. Blyth, Sunderland, Seaham Harbour, Hartlepool and Amble also featured prominently in the booming 'sea coal' trade.

At Blyth, a staith had been opened as early as 1788 on the southern side of the river entrance. This facility was extended by the London and North Eastern Railway in the 1880s. The railway and the Cowpen Coal Company also developed their own staiths on the north side of the river, the last being the West Staiths, which began operation in 1928. At that date the port had four sets of staiths, three of them on the northern bank.

Loading coal at Sunderland Docks c.1950. Sunderland was an important port for shipping County Durham coal.

The development of Blyth as a port was greatly helped by the formation of a harbour commission in 1882 and deepening of the river which had once been notoriously shallow.

At Sunderland, the Hudson Dock, on the south side of the entrance to the Wear, was opened in 1850 and extended in 1855. The Hendon Dock, adjoining the Hudson, was opened in 1868. These docks contained important staiths for loading coal from the County Durham pits, particularly those owned by the wealthy Londonderry family.

Further up the Wear, on the south side, were the Lambton and Hetton staiths, while facing them to the north stood the Wearmouth Staiths. One of the first steam colliers to regularly load at Sunderland was the *Lady Alice Lambton*, built in 1853 and owned by the Earl of Durham. It is possible that she was the first steamer to call at Lambton Staiths (also known as Lambton Drops).

Seaham Harbour was developed in the late 1820s to handle shipments from the 3rd Marquess of Londonderry's County Durham collieries. It began operation in 1831 and was improved over the years, becoming a flourishing port.

Although many of the ships leaving Seaham were bound for London and other southern ports there were also links with Hamburg. The self-discharging steam collier *Herman Sauber* was completed in 1912 by William Doxford at its Pallion yard, Sunderland. She had been ordered by Sauber Brothers of Hamburg for the Seaham Harbour-Hamburg trade.

A unique vessel in her day, the *Herman Sauber*

had a conveyor belt system of discharge patented by Doxford's. With two conveyors working on each side, she was able to discharge up to 1,200 tons of small coal per hour. The cargo could be unloaded in all weathers and covered delivery shoots rendered the process almost dust-free.

Following the First World War the ship was handed over to Britain as part of Germany's reparations, coming under the management of the Pelton Steamship Company of Newcastle. But she was eventually sold back to the Sauber firm.

On October 30 1922 the *Herman Sauber* sailed from Seaham Harbour for Hamburg with coal. By the early morning of November 3 she was encountering heavy seas and her cargo shifted, rendering her unstable. She then capsized and crewmen were thrown into the waves in darkness.

All were lost, except one man who clung to an oar. When daylight came he was picked up eight miles from Spurn Head by a Grimsby trawler. Although utterly exhausted, the man revived and was taken to hospital at Grimsby. The skipper of the trawler reported seeing bodies in the water.

The Sauber Brothers' coal business with the North-East must have stretched back many years for in 1876 another of their steamers, also named the *Herman Sauber*, was described as a regular trader between the Tyne and Hamburg. This *Herman Sauber* became the victim of severe southerly gales in December 1876.

She was on passage from Hamburg to Sunderland to load coal, but when she arrived off the mouth of the Wear her master, a Captain Vogel, considered it was too dangerous to attempt crossing the bar in the heavy seas. With difficulty, he took his ship northwards to the Tyne but again he found the conditions so bad that he would not attempt entering the river.

Forced to stay at sea, the captain took his vessel as far north as

Shipbuilding and Shipping Record

The steam collier Herman Sauber. *She capsized after sailing from Seaham Harbour bound for Hamburg with coal in 1922. Only one man survived.*

the Farne Islands. The weather remained severe, the starboard lifeboat was carried away and the ship's decks were constantly swept by the rough seas.

Provisions were running low, and Captain Vogel decided to make a second attempt to enter the Wear. But yet again he was forced by the raging seas to turn his ship away. The *Herman Sauber* then headed towards the Tyne for a second time. By now it was Christmas Eve and the ship had been battling for nearly six days to make port.

As she attempted to get safely into the river she was struck by a heavy sea which put her steering gear out of action. The *Herman Sauber* was now helpless. She drifted ashore on to rocks at South Shields.

However, the ordeal of those aboard was nearly over. The famous lifeboat *Willie Wouldhave* succeeded in rescuing all her 19 crew. These were lucky men. Four days earlier the steamer *Tyne*, owned by George Otto of North Shields, had sunk near the same spot with the loss of 17 crew.

~U-Boats and Mines~

The outbreak of the First World War in 1914 brought new and terrible dangers for the steam colliers. U-boat attacks and mines took a heavy toll of both ships and men's lives. The colliers were particularly vulnerable because convoys were not introduced along the East Coast until 1918, the last year of the war. Until then, crews braved enormous risks from enemy submarines as they carried out their vital job of delivering coal to the ports of southern England and France. They did this without the protection of warship escorts which a convoy system would have provided.

When the war began in early August 1914 the North-East collier *Sheaf Arrow*, operated by the well known Tyne shipping firm of W.A. Souter, found herself unloading her cargo at Hamburg. The master, Captain T.B. Clarke, realised there was a danger that his ship and her crew would be detained. Fortunately, the steamer was unloaded quickly and she managed to escape from the German port on the same day as her arrival, August 2. The *Sheaf Arrow*, which had been built by the Blyth Shipbuilding and Dry Docks Company in 1912, was almost certainly one of the last British ships to leave.

Eight other North-East colliers in Hamburg were not so lucky. These ships were seized by the Germans and their crews interned. All the vessels had been built at yards on the Tyne, Wear or Blyth. In addition, a ninth ship from the North-East was seized in the port of Harburg, close to Hamburg.

One of the first colliers to be sunk by enemy action during the war was the *Primo*, owned by the Pelton Steam Ship Company of Newcastle. She had been built by Craig Taylor at Stockton in 1898. The vessel was sunk by gunfire from the submarine *U-21* off Cape Antifer on November 26 1914. She

Shipbuilding and Shipping Record

The France, Fenwick collier Portwood, *completed by S.P. Austin of Sunderland in 1913. She survived two U-boat attacks in 1918. In the first attack the torpedo missed but on the second occasion she was hit. Three of her crew were killed. The* Portwood *lived on, but was lost when she was shelled by a U-boat during the early stages of the Second World War in 1939 while sailing for Belgian owners under the name* Suzon.

A collier, probably on her way to load coal at Dunston Staiths, begins to move through the open Swing Bridge. Colliers such as this one had to brave attacks from German U-boats as they delivered coal to ports in the South of England and France during the First World War. In peacetime, a round voyage from the Tyne to London and back might take anything from three to six days. Four-day voyages were common. Another collier, accompanied by a tug, can be seen astern of the first ship, while a sailing vessel is moored at Newcastle Quayside.

was on passage from the Tyne towards Rouen with coal.

The submarine surfaced and came close alongside the *Primo*. A German officer, speaking in excellent English, shouted across from the conning tower. He asked the master of the *Primo*, a Captain Whincop, whether his ship was British. The captain confirmed that she was. He told the officer they were bound for Rouen with coal for the Paris Gas Company.

The U-boat officer suddenly produced a German flag. He informed Captain Whincop that he and his crew would be given exactly five minutes to leave their ship. The captain replied that the *Primo* was a peaceful trader, carrying no arms or contraband of war. But the German officer replied: 'But you are British and my orders are to sink you. War is war.'

Two lifeboats were launched from the collier, one carrying 11 men and the other seven. Captain Whincop was the last to leave the ship. They could see land about six miles away. The sea was fairly rough. When they had rowed about a quarter of a mile from the *Primo*, the U-boat opened fire with her gun. The ship was struck low down on the bows but did not immediately sink. The submarine again fired her gun and this time the collier was set ablaze. Eventually, she slid beneath the waves. But all the crew had survived.

A little over a month later, on December 16 1914, the steamer *Elterwater*, owned by the Elterwater Steam Ship Company of Milburn House, Newcastle, struck a mine believed to have been laid by the German cruiser *Kolberg*.

The *Elterwater*, built by the Blyth S.B. Company, had left the Tyne bound for London with coal earlier that day. Shortly after 6pm, when the ship was three miles off Scarborough, she hit the mine and the resulting explosion blew out the port side of the ship near the engine room. The vessel heeled over and sank by the stern in just a few minutes.

Without time to launch a lifeboat, the surviving crewmen jumped overboard with lifebelts or clung to planks and other objects. They tried to get as far away from the sinking ship as possible to avoid being dragged under by suction.

Fortunately, another ship, the *City*, which had left the Tyne with coal only an hour or two after the *Elterwater*, heard the explosion and saw the ship's lights disappear in the darkness.

The *City*'s master ordered a boat to be launched but the blackness of the night and the amount of wreckage floating in the sea hampered the search for survivors. Luckily, they eventually reached the *Elterwater*'s men who had managed to stay close together. When they were picked up they had been in the water about an hour. The second mate, John Tapping, 35, was lifted into the boat unconscious with a head injury. He died shortly afterwards.

The *City* returned to the Tyne the following day with the 12 survivors of the *Elterwater*. The ship's master, Captain Daniel Gillan, of North Shields, was among them. He had been washed off the bridge as his vessel went down but was picked up. Five men were missing. They were Thomas Digman, the 2nd engineer, of South Shields, Thomas Hoop, the mess room steward, also from South Shields, and three Arab firemen.

The rescue ship *City* had been built at Howdon by Palmer's for the Durham Steam Ship Company of Newcastle in 1892.

Torpedoes from U-boats were as much a threat to the steam colliers as mines. For example, the *Blackwood*, owned by the Tyneside Line of Newcastle, was torpedoed by *U-35* 18 miles south west of Dungeness in the Channel on passage from Blyth to Le Havre with coal on March 9 1915.

The *Blackwood*, under the command of Captain John Souter, had sailed from Blyth two days earlier and encountered rough weather. At 6.10am on March 9 she was attacked by torpedo. The steamer was hit in the fore part of the stokehold on the port side. The saloon was wrecked.

Captain Souter was sleeping in his bunk when the torpedo struck and was awakened by the explosion. He grabbed his clothes and boots and made his way to the upper deck where he quickly dressed. He and the crew of 17 took to the lifeboats. The submarine appeared on the port side of the ship and steamed around the vessel but did not offer assistance to the men in the boats. The *Blackwood* sank half an hour later.

The crew endured cold conditions for three hours in the boats until a fishing vessel picked them up and landed them safely at Newhaven. The *Blackwood* had been built at Blyth by the Blyth S.B. Company in 1907.

The *Lampada*, owned by the Gas Light and Coke Company of London, was another of the many victims of torpedo attack. She had been built by Short Brothers of Sunderland in 1889 and had originally been named the *Snilesworth*.

Under the management of Stephenson Clarke, the *Lampada* had loaded at Felling Staiths on the Tyne with coal for Beckton Gas Works. The ship departed the river on the morning of December 8 1917. The submarine *U-75* attacked her in the afternoon of the same day.

Seaman Matthew Jacobson, from North Shields, was aboard the *Lampada* and wrote down a detailed account of the sinking for posterity in notes about his long seafaring career. He had been lying in his bunk when a tremendous explosion shook the ship. Matthew jumped up and realised they had been torpedoed.

He went on to the open deck and found his fellow crewmen getting a lifeboat ready for launching. Matthew noted that the main engines of the ship were still running at full speed.

Two lifeboats were lowered from the *Lampada*, but the one Matthew Jacobson boarded capsized. The captain was among those thrown into the water. Matthew wrote: 'However, before I realised what was happening I found myself in the water under the boat which was cap-sized. My lungs nearly bursting, I came to the surface and seeing the boat a few yards away I swam slowly towards her and got on the bottom, sitting myself down and trying to make the best of a bad job.

'Only having my underwear on and being soaking wet, I may say my teeth were chattering on that cold day of December 1917. While sitting on the bottom of the upturned boat I saw several of the crew in the water including the captain who I recognised by his bald head. They were all clinging to floating oars and various other things which had been thrown out of the lifeboat when she cap-sized.

'While in this position I saw our ship steaming away in the dis-tance getting deeper and deeper in the water aft. She had been tor-pedoed in No. 3 hold next to the engine room. Finally her stem

An artist's impression of the Lampada *sinking after being torpedoed by a U-boat in December 1917. Matthew Jacobson of North Shields was among the survivors. The ship was built by Short Brothers of Sunderland.*

27

rose in the air and I saw her slide stern first under the water, a small boat floating away from her as she disappeared, with some of the crew pulling towards me. This small boat was always kept handy for any emergency.

'While our small boat was coming towards the upturned boat on which I was sitting, a Norwegian steamer picked them up and shortly after a motor launch came tearing along with great speed and came alongside of our boat. The officer in charge told me to hurry up and jump on board as the submarine, he said, was still somewhere in the vicinity.'

The survivors rescued by the steamer were transferred to this motor boat and landed at Whitby. It appears that Matthew Jacobson was one of the last to be picked up. He was also taken into Whitby aboard the motor boat. He wrote: 'Nearing the quay I looked up and saw a big crowd of people standing on the jetty as we came alongside, the officer in charge telling me to jump ashore. But realising I only had my night underclothes on I asked for the loan of some covering which I promised to bring back right away as soon as I got fixed up ashore.'

The officer took off his overcoat, with gold rings on the cuffs, and put it on Matthew, telling him to bring it back as soon as he got rigged up at the Seamen's Mission. Once at the mission, he met other members of the crew who had been rescued and landed shortly before him.

'Arriving at the mission I was placed before a large fire and supplied with hot coffee and cakes and afterwards fitted out with new clothing and boots. What is more, the missionary took all our home addresses and sent telegrams to our respective homes telling them, 'Ship lost, safe, be home very shortly', which I thought was the essence of kindness.'

Matthew Jacobson then went back to the motor launch to return the officer's coat and thank him. On arriving back at the mission, he learned that two members of the crew were dead and several others missing. In fact, five men had lost their lives.

Matthew continued: 'The kindness of the Missions to Seamen officials did not end there, for we were taken to the railway station and given tickets to take each of us to our homes. Arriving at Newcastle at 2am on Sunday morning and no trains available till 6 or 7 o'clock, I decided to walk down to North Shields, it being a nice clear frosty morning. I soon stepped it out and arrived home in record time.

'My wife, having received the telegram sent from Whitby informing her of the position, was waiting for me with the kettle boiling and after a hot meal asked me if the boy came home with me, meaning the messroom steward, who also belonged to North Shields. I had to tell her he was one of the missing and asked her if, when she had her breakfast, she would go to the boy's home and gently break the news to his mother, a job I couldn't do myself.

Blyth c.1910. A collier loading at Blyth harbour, home of the first steam collier, the Bedlington. The development of the port was greatly helped by the deepening of the river.

'After a quiet day at home on Sunday, and a good night's rest, I rose early next morning and after having breakfast proceeded to the office of Stephenson Clarke, Exchange Buildings, Newcastle, telling them in the office of my predicament and asking what was going to be done. I was told to be at the South Shields Board of Trade Offices on the following Wednesday when I would be paid off.'

At South Shields, Matthew met up with the rest of the surviving crew members, including the captain. Good humouredly, he told the captain he had recognised him in the water by his bald head. They all received three weeks wages and were signed off.

The Tyne-built *Fulgens*, the first ship to be owned by the Gas Light and Coke Company, was among the many other colliers sunk during the war. She was torpedoed by the German submarine *UB-10* near the Haisborough Light Vessel off the Norfolk coast on August 1 1915. The crew survived.

However, aboard some ships loss of life was heavy. For example, the *Dauntless*, completed by the Blyth S.B. Company in 1897, was sunk by the submarine *UB-39* off Le Coubre Point, France, in February 1917. She had been on a voyage from the Tyne to Bayonne with coal. Fifteen of her crew died.

The *Phare*, a Gas Light and Coke Company vessel also constructed by the Blyth S.B. Company, lost 14 men killed when she was torpedoed and sunk by *UB-35*, less than three miles North-East of Scarborough, on October 31 1917. The *Phare* had been taking coal from the Tyne to London.

Sometimes the war might come very close to the North-East coast. For example, the *Flamma*, a new ship built by Wood Skinner of Bill Quay, had been in service barely a month when she hit a mine off Seaham Harbour on July 10 1917 as she made her way towards the Tyne in ballast. The *Flamma* was run on to the beach

A Duncan, Gravesend

Survivor. The Gas Light and Coke Company's Flamma. *She hit a mine off Seaham Harbour in July 1917 while on her way to the Tyne in ballast. The* Flamma *survived and received a new bow section at the Wood Skinner shipyard, Bill Quay, Gateshead, where she had been built.*

north of Hartlepool and later towed back to the Bill Quay yard where she was given a new bow section. She then returned to service.

The *Firelight*, built by J. Blumer at Sunderland in 1896, was torpedoed and sunk by the German submarine *UC-29* on May 1 1917 less than two miles east of the Tyne piers. This happened shortly after the *Firelight* had left the river bound for London. But her crew were among the lucky ones – they were all saved.

During the First World War 166 seamen lost their lives through enemy action while sailing with coal from the Tyne, Wear and Blyth to the South of England, French Channel and Bay of Biscay ports. To this figure must be added those lost returning northwards in ballast. All these unfortunate men and their surviving shipmates had braved extreme dangers to deliver their cargoes of black diamonds. Their courageous service should not be forgotten.

~Rescue and Loss~

On December 5 1929 the Tyne-built collier *Frances Duncan* was steaming off Land's End, Cornwall, in very rough seas when she was struck by an immense wave on the starboard side. The blow caused her cargo of coal to shift and the vessel heeled over on to her side. Her decks were now virtually perpendicular to the sea.

It was impossible to successfully launch the two lifeboats which overturned because of the heavy list to port. The steep slope of the

decks also stopped the radio operator from gaining access to the wireless cabin.

The *Frances Duncan* remained on her side, known to mariners as her 'beam ends', for about half an hour and then turned turtle. Crewmen were thrown into the sea, but four of them managed to cling to the upturned bottom of their ship. Huge waves constantly threatened to wash them off.

The master of the *Frances Duncan*, Captain F. Martin, was the last to leave the vessel, but he could not swim. Luckily, he managed to hold on to a piece of wreckage and by a miracle of fate the wreckage was washed close to the upturned steamer. The crewmen hauled the captain on to it.

They had been in the water for about half an hour when the Newcastle steam collier *Alice Marie* appeared on the scene. She was taking a cargo of coal from Barry, Glamorgan, to Norway. Her master, Captain C.W. Blaylock, of South Shields, steamed to the rescue despite the heavy seas, displaying magnificent seamanship. At one point his vessel came perilously close to the rocks of The Longships Light but by expertly handling his ship he saved five lives.

The first man rescued was picked up from an upturned lifeboat. Then the *Alice Marie* threw a line to one of the crew clinging to the overturned ship. The man

Watercolour by W.H. Forster, 1923, owned by Dick Keys

Saved lives. A painting of the Alice Marie. *The ship was completed by S.P. Austin at Sunderland in 1920 for the Rodney Steamship Company of Newcastle. She rescued five men from the collier* Frances Duncan.

caught it and was hauled through the raging seas to safety. Next it was the turn of Captain Martin to be rescued. He too made it safely to the decks of the *Alice Marie*. Finally, two more men were picked up, including the wireless operator.

The rescue ship sighted another member of the crew clinging to some wreckage and Captain Blaylock manoeuvred his vessel towards him. However, on reaching the wreckage he found the unfortunate man had vanished. The *Alice Marie* landed the five survivors of the 21-man crew at Brixham. Those lost included all the engineers who were likely to have been trapped below decks.

The *Frances Duncan*, which had been taking a cargo of coal from Cardiff to Rouen, sank and wreckage was washed ashore at Sennen Cove, Cornwall. The ship had been completed by Palmer's of Jarrow in 1907.

The courage of the *Alice Marie*'s Captain Blaylock and his men was beyond doubt. The master had taken a calculated risk to save lives, but his steamer could have suffered a similar fate to the *Frances Duncan* or have struck the rocks.

The *Alice Marie* had been built at Sunderland by S.P. Austin, being completed in 1920. Her owners were the Rodney Steamship Company of Newcastle.

Nearly all her 20-man and one-woman crew at the time of the rescue were from Tyneside or other areas of the North-East. The list included men from South Shields, North Shields, Newcastle, Gateshead, Jarrow, Cleadon, Seaham Harbour and West Hartlepool. The one woman was the captain's wife, Lilian Blaylock, who had been signed on as a stewardess.

In January 1930, Captain Blaylock and the ship's carpenter William Stokes received awards for their courage and skill. The captain was presented with a silver salver by the Cardiff and Bristol Channel Shipowners' Association 'in recognition of the seamanship displayed in saving five lives of the crew of the S.S. *Frances Duncan*, which foundered off Land's End in the exceptionally heavy weather experienced on December 5, 1929'.

J.T. Duncan of Cardiff, the managing owners of the *Frances Duncan*, presented the captain with a gold watch and Carpenter

Stokes with a silver watch. In addition, both received Lloyd's Medals.

As well as this brave rescue, the period between the two world wars also saw the disappearance of two colliers. The first was the *Adderstone*, owned by Alexander Brothers of Newcastle.

The ship was only a year old when she sailed from Dunston Staiths with coal for Hamburg on December 30 1921. Her crew numbered 19. Six of them were from Tyneside, including a father and son. The *Adderstone* failed to arrive at the German port.

On November 19 1935 the *Sheaf Brook*, owned by the Sheaf Steam Shipping Company of Newcastle, sailed from Springwell

Rescue award. Carpenter William Stokes of the Alice Marie *receives the Lloyd's Bronze Medal for his part in the rescue of crewmen from the* Frances Duncan *off Land's End in 1929. The* Alice Marie's *master, Captain C.W. Blaylock, of South Shields, received the Lloyd's Silver Medal.*

Staiths, Jarrow, also bound for Hamburg with black diamonds. She was carrying a crew of 20, most of them from Tyneside.

The following day the *Sheaf Brook* sent out an S.O.S. message for help when 110 miles east-south-east of the Tyne. The radio message included the information: 'Require assistance. Cabin flooded. Dangerous list to port.'

The S.O.S. prompted a sister ship, the *Sheaf Water*, into immediate action. She steamed at full speed to the position given by the vessel in distress. Meanwhile, the tug *Superman* had put out from Hull in the hope of assisting.

When the *Sheaf Water* reached the reported position of the *Sheaf Brook* there was no ship to be seen but she sighted an upturned lifeboat and floating wreckage. Three rockets were seen to the north-north-west.

The *Sheaf Water* continued the search in the direction of the rockets

Ships crowd the basin at Dunston Staiths on the Tyne, c.1920. Dunston was one of the river's most important coal loading points. The first of these staiths opened in 1893. A second set of staiths was added to the facility in 1903. At Dunston, the loading of ships from the six berths could be undertaken at any stage of the tide, a tribute to the dredging work of the Tyne Improvement Commission.

and sent out the radio message: 'Have sighted three rockets. If you hear our wireless send up more rockets.' But no more were seen.

The missing ship's master was Captain C.E. Brown, of Jesmond, Newcastle, who had a wife and one child. It was the first ship he had commanded.

The mate, M. Peterson, of South Shields, had served in the *Sheaf Brook* for six months and had survived being torpedoed during the First World War. The third engineer, W. Richardson, also of South Shields, was the father of two boys.

Able Seaman W. Sloten, from Tyne Dock, had only recently joined the vessel after being unemployed for eight months. He had a wife and three children. Steward R. Hodgson, of South Shields, had a wife and two children. Also lost was mess room boy A.E. Wharrier, of Dunston.

The North Sea had claimed the lives of another collier crew.

~The Alley of Danger~

The Second World War again brought the constant danger of enemy attack to the colliers off the East Coast and in the Channel. This time, however, convoys were introduced from the start of the conflict in 1939 and continued until the end in 1945.

The ships carrying coal now faced a new threat in the shape of Germany's fast motor torpedo boats, known to the British as E-boats, but to the Germans as Schnellboot (fast boats). Their German name was entirely accurate, for they could travel at around 40 knots, a speed which enabled them to escape nearly all pursuing vessels.

Armed with guns and torpedoes, and capable of laying mines, the E-boats operated at night, attacking ships on the route between the coalfields of the North-East and the ports of the South. In addition to this formidable menace, the colliers also faced attacks from enemy dive-bombers and, in the narrow Straits of Dover, the heavy guns of shore batteries firing from German-occupied France. As in the First World War, mines too were an ever present danger, and they were more sophisticated. Acoustic and magnetic types were introduced.

Southbound convoys started with the assembly of a few merchant vessels and their escorts off Methil on the northern shore of the Firth of Forth. The escort ships might include corvettes, anti-submarine trawlers, sloops and veteran destroyers or light cruisers. Although at first largely unarmed, as the war progressed the merchant vessels were equipped with small guns which were generally mounted aft.

As it moved southwards, a convoy would be joined by other merchant ships from ports along the East Coast. Not surprisingly, a large number joined from the Blyth, Tyne and Wear. By the time a convoy had passed Hull it might number 50 or more vessels.

The channel which the convoys followed through the protective East Coast minefields was marked by buoys displaying red lights. This busy but hazardous shipping lane was swept of mines on a daily basis. German aircraft, E-boats and submarines could all lay these lethal devices. British mines could also be a danger. The section of the route off the coasts of Norfolk and Suffolk between the Sheringham Buoy and the Shipwash Light Vessel became known as 'E-boat Alley', so notorious was its reputation for attacks. Operating in darkness, the E-boats were known on occasions to tie up at the buoys and await the arrival of a convoy. Sometimes they would strike with torpedoes from the landward side of the channel.

These deadly craft favoured nights when visibility was poor and the sea active enough to disguise their bow waves. In addition to their high-speed diesel engines, they were also equipped with quiet, slow-running motors which proved impossible to hear from the decks of ships in the convoy. By switching to these motors they were able to cruise at low speed, stalking their prey.

E-boats were thus difficult to detect, elusive and stealthy. With their shallow draft, they could escape across the minefields at high speed if fired on.

The first East Coast collier to be sunk during the war was William France, Fenwick's *Goodwood*, completed by S.P Austin at Sunderland in 1937. On September 9 1939 she was badly damaged by a mine off Flamborough Head while sailing in convoy from the Tyne towards Bayonne with coal.

The ship's captain had both his legs broken when he was blown off the bridge on to the foredeck by the explosion. He ordered the crew to abandon ship. They obeyed the order, but two men returned to the vessel to save him. As the *Goodwood* was sinking rapidly they had little choice but to throw their captain into the

Lieutenant Commander Michael Irwin (RNVR, Retired), of Gosforth, Newcastle, who served in East Coast convoys during the Second World War.

water. He was then taken aboard one of the lifeboats and survived. The mine which sank his ship had been laid by a U-boat.

Soon, however, E-boats as well as mines began sinking ships. On July 27 1940 three E-boats attacked and sank three British vessels in the Channel off Shoreham. The victims included the *Broadhurst*, bound from Seaham to Shoreham, and the *London Trader*, on passage from the Tyne to Shoreham. Both were carrying coal. The *Broadhurst* lost four men and the *London Trader* one.

On September 23 of the same year another trio of E-boats launched a deadly attack. this time in E-boat Alley near Haisborough Sands. The collier *Joseph Swan* lost 15 crewmen dead

when she was torpedoed and sunk. She had been bound from Blyth to London with coal. The *Corbrook*, *New Lambton*, *Nieuwland* and *Fulham V* were also sent to the bottom by torpedoes. The *Fulham V* was bound from the Tyne to London with 2,300 tons of coal.

Michael Irwin, of Gosforth, Newcastle, was an officer in the Royal Naval Volunteer Reserve during the war. He served in the sloop HMS *Lowestoft* as a young Sub-Lieutenant in the East Coast convoys in 1940.

Michael remembers vividly the sinking of the *N.C. Monberg*, a Danish ship serving under the British flag, on December 15 of that year. She had been carrying 3,000 tons of coal from the Tyne to London. The *Lowestoft* was engaged in escorting the convoy and the warship had just passed the Smith's Knoll Light off Suffolk when an explosion was observed far astern.

He wrote a number of years later: 'The convoy sailed from Methil but owing to very bad weather it had to put into the Tyne for shelter. Our hopes of a night ashore were soon shattered for the Tyne portion of the convoy had sailed and we were ordered to catch it up off Flamborough Head.

'The seas became calmer as we proceeded south and two nights later the waters were glassy calm. The moon shone through the night haze. It was the sort of night when everyone is at peace with the world. I for one did not contemplate danger as the buoys with their lights flashing passed by.

'We had just passed a buoy about 600 yards to port and I was about to put the position on the chart when the Asdic operator reported hydrophone effect on his set. He stated it was a fast moving craft on the surface. It could only mean either one of our own coastal craft returning from operations or an enemy boat.

'Events moved quickly. Within a few seconds there was an explosion at the rear of the convoy. A few minutes later one of the escort came alongside and reported that a ship had been torpedoed. It seemed likely that the enemy had secured to the buoy with engines stopped and allowed the leading ships of the convoy to pass before carrying out its successful attack.'

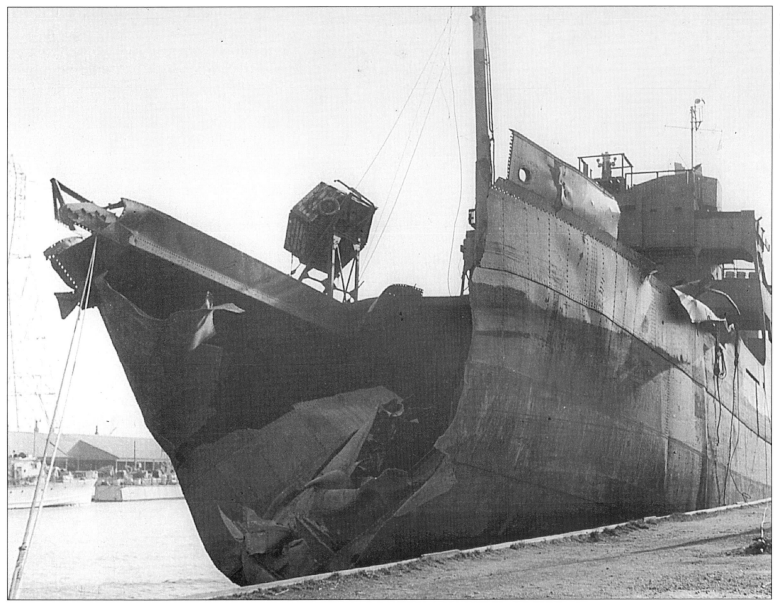

E-boat victim. The Firelight, *owned by the Gas Light and Coke Company, showing her badly damaged bows. She was torpedoed by an E-boat in 1943 but survived and was repaired at Readhead's shipyard, South Shields.*

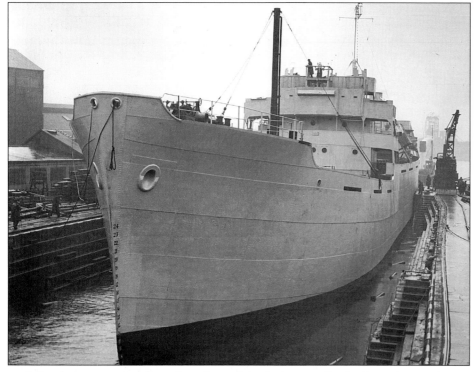

Firelight *after repairs. She is being floated out of dry dock at Readhead's shipyard in April 1944.*

The vessels sunk included the *Corduff*, bound from London to Hartlepool in ballast. Seven of the crew lost their lives and two wounded men were taken prisoner by the E-boat which had torpedoed them. Fourteen, including the *Corduff's* captain, were rescued by the Cromer lifeboat.

Eight men died when the *Togston*, bound from Blyth to London with 2,200 tons of coal, was torpedoed and sunk in the Alley on the same night. Eleven of the crew were picked up by the corvette HMS *Puffin*. The following month the E-boats were again in action against a convoy in the Alley. On April 4 they sank two ships and damaged another off Corton, north Suffolk. One of the vessels sent to the bottom was the *Effra*, bound from the Tyne to London with 1,300 tons of coke. Two men were lost.

November 1941 saw two more colliers torpedoed and sunk by the feared German craft. They were the *Aruba*, sailing from Blyth to Cowes with 1,750 tons of coal, and the *Waldinge*, on passage from the Tyne to London with 4,100 tons of black diamonds. Each ship lost one man.

However, vessels sometimes survived torpedo attack, staying afloat against all the odds and being towed into port for repairs. They included the *Dalewood*, a France, Fenwick collier, which suffered major damage when she was torpedoed by an E-boat in August 1941. Her engine room was wrecked by the attack but she refused to go down. The *Dalewood* was towed to safety and underwent major repairs. Afterwards, she resumed service and was not broken up until 1972.

Another ship which came through the ordeal of war to serve in peace time was the *Firelight*, the second of the Gas Light and Coke Company's vessels to bear that name. She was hit by an E-boat torpedo while sailing between Cromer and Great Yarmouth in 1943. Her bow section began sinking. The convoy escort ships fired starshells and opened up their guns on the German raider.

The victim of the ambush was the *N.C. Monberg*, which had been torpedoed by an E-boat with the loss of 12 lives. Although a Danish ship, the crew had been mainly British. By a strange coincidence, Michael had sailed in this vessel between France and the Tyne before the war. Sub-Lieutenant Irwin went on to attain the rank of Lieutenant Commander. He commanded landing craft on D-day as well as serving at Salerno and in midget submarines. Michael also served in a Q-ship disguised as a German blockade runner off Norway in 1942.

One of the worst attacks in E-boat Alley took place on March 7 1941 when two convoys passing each other off the coast of Norfolk suffered the loss of seven ships. Fifty-four seamen were killed.

The *Firelight* managed to keep afloat because a sturdy bulkhead resisted the pressure of the sea, though there were anxious moments when it seemed to her master, Captain Thomas West, of South Shields, that the bulkhead might give way.

The ship's engines were off and at one point she drifted near the coastal sands and towards a mined area. However, her engines were restarted and she slowly moved away from these dangers, rejoining the shipping lane. Two tugs came to her aid and *Firelight* was towed to South Shields where she was drydocked and repaired. The vessel's crew all lived to tell the tale.

Also a survivor was the *Wandle*, owned by the Wandsworth & District Gas Company. This flat-iron collier was torpedoed off Lowestoft on November 9 1942 on a ballast passage northwards to the Tyne. She too was repaired at South Shields and after the war re-entered service on the Tyne-London run, delivering supplies to the Wandsworth Gas Works, far up the Thames.

Stephenson Clarke Shipping Ltd.

The Gasfire *was attacked and her after-section badly damaged in October 1940. She was towed to S.P. Austin's yard on the River Wear at Sunderland where the after-section was rebuilt. In this picture the repairs are nearly complete. The* Gasfire *had been built by S.P. Austin, being launched into the Wear in 1936.*

By a strange quirk of fate the last France, Fenwick collier to be sunk during the conflict was the replacement for the first to be sunk. Both were named the *Goodwood* and both were built by S.P Austin at Sunderland. The second *Goodwood* was torpedoed by an E-boat off Lowestoft on February 22 1945 while sailing from Blyth to London. She had been commanded by Sunderland-born Captain T.N. Beaton. Her 21 crew and five gunners survived.

The E-boats remained a threat to British East Coast shipping throughout the war. As late as March 19 1945 they sent the Stephenson Clarke collier *Rogate* to the bottom with the loss of two men. The attack took place off Corton while the *Rogate* was on passage from Sunderland to London with 4,000 tons of coal.

A total of 267 men lost their lives in the Second World War on the East Coast coal runs southwards from the Tyne, Wear and Blyth to South of England and French Channel ports. Many were also lost in the northbound convoys. Once again, the collier crewmen, most of them from the North-East, had shown bravery of a high order to keep gas works and power stations supplied with black diamonds.

~Wrecked on the Sands~

The Second World War also witnessed an accident on the East Coast run which had nothing to do with raids by the enemy. On August 6 1941, while steaming in convoy, the escort trawler *Agate* unwittingly led seven merchant ships on to the treacherous Haisborough Sands off the Norfolk coast as dawn broke.

They had encountered misty conditions and a gale blowing from the north-north-west, accompanied by rain. The mist appears to have been a major factor in the disaster. The convoy had been unable to see the Haisborough Light which because of wartime restrictions only operated at pre-arranged times for about 10 minutes when a convoy was due to pass.

Running aground on the sands was dangerous enough, but the stranded vessels, most of them colliers, suffered the further blow of being pounded by the gale-driven seas until they became hopeless wrecks.

Fortunately the masters of several other ships, which had also been following the *Agate*, escaped the same fate. They realised their vessels would be on a danger course towards the notorious sands. They refused to carry on and saved their ships from the perils of Haisborough.

The seven vessels which ran aground included the *Taara*, which had been built by S.P. Austin, of Sunderland, as the *Fleetwing*. She had been one of the colliers seized in German ports at the start of the First World War. The *Fleetwing* was later sold to Estonian owners and renamed the *Taara*.

Among the other ships wrecked was the *Gallois*, sailing under French ownership. She had been completed by Wood Skinner of Bill Quay in 1917 as the *Tynemouth* for the Burnett Steamship Company of Newcastle. Also lost was the *Deerwood*, a France,

Fenwick collier completed in 1920 by J. Crown & Sons of Sunderland. She had been on passage from Blyth to London with coal.

A new S.P. Austin-built ship, the *Betty Hindley*, which had just started her career with Stephenson Clarke, also came to grief. She had been launched into the Wear only two months before she went aground. Other ships lost were the *Afon Towey*, *Oxshott*, and *Aberhill*.

Braving the hazards of the sands and gale, a pair of lifeboats from Cromer and one from Gorleston, together with the anti-submarine trawler *Bassett* and a boat from a destroyer, saved many men from the stranded ships.

One of the Cromer lifeboats was commanded by the famous RNLI coxswain Henry Blogg. When he reached the scene he found two of the ships partly submerged. During the rescue operation, Blogg's boat was badly damaged as it bumped and scraped against submerged sections of the wrecks and at one point momentarily grounded on the sands, but he and his crew succeeded in rescuing 88 men from four of the vessels.

The three lifeboats saved a total of 119 lives. Coxswain Blogg transferred the seamen he rescued to destroyers whose officers had watched in admiration as the lifeboats went into action.

The list of men lost included nine from the *Afon Towey*, two from the *Deerwood*, one from the *Gallois* and two from the *Taara*.

The war also saw the disappearance of a ship in a southbound convoy. The vessel was the *Pacific*, owned by the Williamstown Shipping Company Ltd., of London, which left Sunderland with a cargo of coal for the capital on February 7 1943. Her crew numbered 38.

The night of February 8-9 brought rough conditions with a

gale blowing from the south-south-west and the ships of the convoy became scattered. It was reported that a man was washed overboard from the steamer *Hoogkerk*. When dawn broke the *Pacific* and two other vessels had disappeared from the convoy.

The two unnamed ships may have managed to rejoin the convoy or reach port, but it was confirmed later that the *Pacific* had vanished without trace along with her crew. Her exact fate has never been known but it was thought that the ship sank in the heavy seas before any distress signals could be put out. The gales experienced during the passage of this convoy were among the worst that winter.

An artist's impression of the Deerwood *and two other colliers aground on Haisborough Sands in 1941. Mist is likely to have been a major factor in the disaster. Many crewmen were rescued by Norfolk lifeboats. In all, eight vessels ran aground, including an escort trawler.*

However, the body of a gunner from the *Pacific* was found on the shore near Egmond, Holland, on February 21 that year. It was also reported that an unidentified wreck had been discovered in the North Sea, in position 52.55.8 North, 1.30.37 East, which may have been that of the ill-fated *Pacific*.

~Seamen Look Back~

ilson Glanville was a seaman who sailed in steam colliers during the Second World War. Born in Walker, Newcastle, he served his apprenticeship in general cargo ships, first going to sea at the age of 15. He joined his first collier in 1940. He had married a farmer's daughter and his home was at Ovington in the Tyne Valley, Northumberland. It is perhaps not surprising that the crews he sailed with nicknamed him 'the farmer's boy'.

Wilson recalled that the majority of men in the colliers were from Tyneside or other parts of the North-East. He was by no means always in the watch ashore crew when his ship moored in the Tyne or Wear. Often he would have to remain aboard and was

unable to return to his home, particularly as he had a considerable distance to travel to Ovington. He only got ashore about three times out of 10. Looking back, he considered the Tyne to be the easiest of the North-East ports to enter, although all had their difficulties. Seaham Harbour with its narrow entrance took the accolade for the most difficult and was nicknamed by some crews 'the hole in the wall'. He recalled that in a four-hold ship, No 2 and 3 holds amidships were loaded to their capacity. No 1 hold, at the fore end of the vessel, was never completely filled to avoid the ship being 'down by the head' when at sea.

Wilson sailed through E-boat Alley many times and was lucky enough to come through unscathed. When he first began sailing this hazardous route few of the colliers had any guns. They went out from the ports of the North-East unarmed. To Wilson the ships were 'like sitting ducks'.

He remembered his ship being attacked by a German dive-bomber shortly after she left the Tyne fully loaded, in company with other colliers. They were waiting off the river to join a convoy from Methil when the aircraft came in from the east. Wilson's ship was machine-gunned by the plane, which also dropped a bomb, luckily missing the vessel. However, another collier was sunk in the attack. He was told the bomb had been dropped down the ship's funnel.

'We manned the Lewis gun and had a few shots at him,' he said. 'The pilot

Seaham Harbour c.1935. The harbour was nicknamed 'the hole in the wall' because of its narrow outer entrance. It was particularly difficult to enter when north-easterly winds were blowing.

came so low I could see him in the cockpit. He was wearing a black helmet.' Wilson's ship on this occasion was likely to have been the *Brinkburn*. 'After such attacks you just breathed a sigh of relief and went on with the job,' he added.

Mines came close to the ships he sailed in on several occasions. In his view they were often in more danger from British mines than the enemy's. Bad weather could set them adrift.

Wilson had started the war as an Able Seaman, by the time it had ended he was a First Mate.

Sammy Allen, of Jarrow, who was born and brought up in South Shields, first went to sea with his father at the age of nine. His two-month spell in the Cory steam collier *Cookham* gave him a taste of life aboard ship at an early age.

Not surprisingly, he followed in his father's footsteps as a sea-farer when he grew up. He also followed in his mother's footsteps – she was a stewardess aboard Bergen Line ferries sailing between Newcastle and Norway.

Sammy served as a steward in Stephenson Clarke colliers for 44 years. His first ship was the *Keynes*, an old-style collier with her engines sited amidships. He joined her in 1926. She was frequently engaged in taking coal from Lambton Drops on the Wear to a glass works in Cork, Ireland.

He was still a steward aboard the *Keynes* when she was sunk by aircraft attack off the Lincolnshire coast on January 11 1940. They had delivered their cargo to Southampton and were returning northwards to Sunderland in ballast when a German dive-bomber came in from seawards.

Sammy was in the ship's galley making tea at the time. A bomb hit the vessel amidships, tearing open deck plating and blowing the port lifeboat to pieces. The bunkers were set on fire. 'On hearing the explosion I left the galley and went below to try to find the ship's cat,' he said. 'But I couldn't find the animal and went on deck where the crew were having difficulty launching the remaining lifeboat as the ship was listing heavily.'

However, the boat was eventually launched with all the crew, including the captain, safely aboard. Three men were injured. The

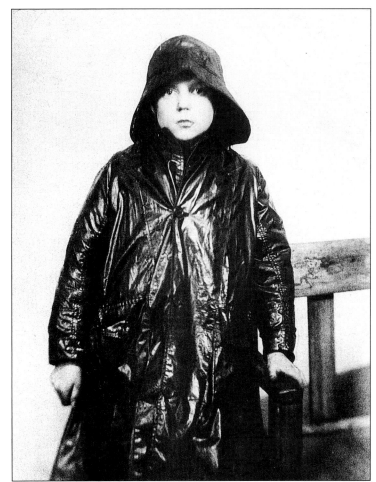

Sammy Allen

Sammy Allen, from South Shields, at the age of nine, when he spent two months at sea aboard the collier Cookham *in which his father was serving.*

wireless operator had received shrapnel wounds from the bomb, which had dropped next to his cabin on the port side. In addition, one of the seamen broke a leg when he fell from the bridge steps as the ship was being evacuated and another man burned his hands as he slid down a rope to the lifeboat.

They waited for an hour or so and were then picked up by the

Sammy Allen, from South Shields, who was a steward in Stephenson Clarke colliers for 44 years, and the Keynes, *the ship in which he served until she was sunk by a bomb attack in 1940. All the crew managed to escape in a lifeboat. The* Keynes *is pictured in 1926 at Cork, the year Sammy joined her.*

destroyer HMS *Jackal* which took them to Grimsby. Luckily the weather had been unusually calm for a January day, although Sammy recalled that it was cold. The three injured men were taken to hospital. The rest of the crew, including Sammy, went to a seamen's mission where they were given tea. The skipper handed each of the men £5, which was two weeks' wages. They could return home or find accommodation if they wished. Sammy decided to return to South Shields by train. It was not long before he had joined another Stephenson Clarke ship, the *Nephrite*, which had previously sailed for Scottish owners. All the 17 crew of the *Keynes* had survived and 10 of them joined the *Nephrite*, a smaller vessel without a wireless.

Len Slater, of North Shields, who was born at Whitley Bay, served as an Ordinary Seaman in a former French-owned collier, the *SNA10*, in 1941 at the age of 16, signing on at North Shields. He recalled the time when a German aircraft dropped a bomb on his ship's forecastle which failed to explode. The ship still had to continue in the convoy but the bomb was eventually removed off Southend.

Len remembered sighting E-boats escaping at high speed across the minefields and saw torpedoed foreign seamen in the water calling out at dusk off Haisborough Sands. The torpedoed ship had been ahead of his when attacked.

'I will never forget these poor men calling out. They were shouting 'English, English',' he said. 'I wanted to throw them a line or stop the ship. But I was told that if any man caught the line he would be sucked towards our propellers.'

Len also pointed out that the merchant ships of the convoy were under orders not to stop. He felt that it was likely the seamen in the water were picked up by one of the Royal Navy escort vessels at the rear of the convoy. A ship was generally designated for the task of rescue.

On another occasion, while serving in a different vessel, a dive-bomber attacked them out of the blue off Flamborough Head. The plane veered away as suddenly as it had appeared and the ship's gunners had no time to return fire. Luckily, the crew escaped the encounter without injury.

~Torpedo in the Night~

Stan Bryson, of Gateshead, was a merchant seaman for most of his working life, serving in deep sea ships as well as colliers. He joined his first vessel as she lay in the Tyne in 1935. The ship loaded coal at Dunston for Port Said, Egypt. His first job was as a galley boy. Stan helped to rescue 14 men from the torpedoed collier *Kenton* on March 7 1941. This errand of mercy proved to be almost as much of an ordeal for the rescuers as for the survivors.

His ship at this time was the France, Fenwick collier *Kentwood*, which had been completed at the yard of Sir John Laing, Sunderland, in 1924. The *Kenton* was owned by Michael Whitaker of Newcastle, and had been completed under a different name in 1913 by Osborne Graham & Co, also of Sunderland.

The *Kenton* and *Kentwood* were at the rear of a northbound convoy when an E-boat launched an attack shortly after 10pm. As usual, they had no inkling that the craft was lurking somewhere out in the darkness on the edge of the narrow channel.

Stan had just finished a two-hour spell at the wheel of the *Kentwood* and went down to the galley for a mug of coffee. He then lay down for some rest, using his lifejacket as a makeshift pillow. Shortly afterwards, he heard an explosion, the force of the blast causing the ship to momentarily heel over. Stan thought his vessel had been hit by a torpedo.

He sprang up and went on deck where the captain gave the order to clear the starboard lifeboat which was already swung out in case of emergencies. At this point Stan still thought his ship had been hit and might be sinking. However, the E-boat torpedo had missed them and had struck the *Kenton*, which was close by. Survivors from the *Kenton* managed to board a lifeboat, but it was damaged during the launch and became waterlogged. Meanwhile, Stan and four other crew members of the *Kentwood* volunteered to

Stan Bryson

Stan Bryson, of Gateshead, who served in colliers as well as deep sea ships. While an Able Seaman aboard France, Fenwick's Kentwood *in 1941 he took part in the rescue of survivors from the collier* Kenton *which had been torpedoed by an E-boat.*

man their own lifeboat in an attempt to rescue these men. He recalled that besides himself, the volunteers were a Chief Officer Martin, from South Shields, the ship's gunner, a mess boy from South Shields and an Able Seaman from Newfoundland.

The lowering of their lifeboat did not go well. During its descent of the ship's side it tilted because of a problem with one of the ropes and the five men were nearly tipped into the sea. Then, when the boat reached the water it drifted towards the stern, coming perilously close to the propellers which were still revolving at full speed. They would learn later that the captain had decided to steam onwards because he believed E-boats might still be in the area. The rescue crew shouted out for the engines to be stopped and at the same time the men from the *Kenton* were also calling out for help. In the confusion tracer shots were fired at the rescuers, possibly from a British ship.

The German attack had come from the landward side of the swept channel and Stan saw the white streak thrown up by an E-boat as it escaped seawards.

The rescuers managed to pull away from the stern and begin their task. The men in the *Kenton*'s boat were wearing lifejackets fitted with battery-operated lights and blowing whistles. This enabled the rescuers to locate them in the darkness.

When the *Kentwood*'s men reached the 14 survivors they found 13 of them standing in the water of their flooded boat. One of the men was unable to stand. He was the captain of the *Kenton*, who had been badly wounded in both legs.

The rescuers transferred the 14 to their boat. The *Kentwood*'s men pulled towards the stricken ship as it gradually sank by the stern An Arab stoker was on the bridge, but he would not jump into the water despite being urged to do so. He disappeared and they were unable to save him. The boat crew then rowed around to the other side of the *Kenton*, but they could see no-one in the water.

Stan learned that his counterpart on the *Kenton*, a man who had also just finished a spell at the wheel, had been trapped when the galley stove fell on top of him as the vessel began to sink. He was among those lost.

However, the problems of that eventful night were not yet over. Those in the boat had to endure a long wait of four to five hours for the *Kentwood* to return. It was a further ordeal for the survivors who were in a state of shock and an uncomfortable experience for the rescue boat crew. However, at last they saw a light flashing. The ship was coming back. They responded by flashing a torch.

The attack had taken place shortly after 10pm. It was between 3am and 4am before the ship returned to pick them up. The survivors were given warm clothing by the *Kentwood*'s crew and the captain decided to land them at Hull. Four men from the *Kenton* had lost their lives. 'It could have been us,' commented Stan many years later. 'The torpedo which hit the *Kenton* was probably intended for our ship as we were the bigger vessel.'

When not far from Spurn Head, at the entrance to the Humber, the ship met an armed trawler serving with the Royal Navy. She signalled to the *Kentwood* to stop her engines and told them they were entering a minefield. 'Luckily we were a light ship, in ballast,' said Stan. 'If we had been loaded with coal we might well have detonated a submerged mine.'

The trawler gave the *Kentwood* a safe course up the Humber. All aboard must have been weary with the trauma and anxieties of the night. When they reached Hull an ambulance arrived at the quayside to take the wounded captain of the *Kenton* to hospital. Stan never got to learn whether he lived or died.

A Royal Navy van also arrived and took other survivors to the Flying Angel Mission of the Shipwrecked Seamen's Society in Hull, where they were given clothes, money and travel warrants to return home. Here they found a haven of comfort and friendly warmth far removed from the shocks of war they had so recently endured.

The *Kentwood* then waited for several days in port before she was able to join another northbound convoy.

The rescue ship's luck in avoiding the perils of conflict did not last. Later in the war she struck a mine and was lost off the Humber. All the crew were rescued. But Stan was not among them. He had left the *Kentwood* three weeks before she was wrecked and by that time had joined another ship.

Stan went on to become a boatswain, serving in this key job aboard various ships for 17 years. When he retired in 1982 he had been a seaman for over 42 years.

The Audun, completed in Norway in 1925, passes through the Tyne's Swing Bridge, c.1945. World War II-style liferafts are fitted to her. The ship's forehatches are covered in coal. The busiest year for the Swing Bridge was in 1924 when 6,007 vessels passed through. A collier approaching the bridge would signal it to open by blowing her steam whistle three times.

~The Last Cargo~

The discovery of natural gas, which ended the need for coal supplies to gas works, and the increasing use of oil by power stations contributed to the decline of the collier on the East Coast run.

On March 20 1998 the *Lord Citrine* became the last collier to leave the Tyne with a cargo of black diamonds. She was loaded with 21,544 tonnes at Tyne Dock for delivery to King's North Power Station on the Medway in Kent. Her cargo was more than 20 times the amount of that carried by the pioneering *John Bowes* in 1852, an indication of the increase in the size of ships engaged in the trade over 150 years.

The *Lord Citrine*'s departure marked the end of an era. The Tyne's famous export of 'sea coal' had stretched back for centuries. Black diamonds were carried from the river in sailing ships, then in steamers, and during the last decades in motor vessels.

Won from the underground seams of Northumberland and County Durham by the arduous labour of generations of miners, this most unassuming of precious stones was dusty and without sparkle but provided communities with their heating and lighting, keeping factories, gas works, power stations, ships and locomotives running in war and peace.

However, to view the last sailing as a final one would perhaps be unwise. As long as coal exists beneath the surface of the North-East it is not beyond the realms of possibility that this once greatly sought after commodity will one day again be shipped from the Tyne and other rivers of the region. But it must be admitted that at the present time such a revival appears unlikely.

The men of the North-East coal ships had kept the gas works and power stations of London and the South running, delivering their supplies even in the most difficult of circumstances. They deserve our admiration for their courage in the face of the elements and the extreme dangers of wartime.

Today, looking out towards the sea from Tynemouth or South Shields, it is easy to imagine the warm feelings of a Geordie collierman as his ship entered the Tyne, finding refuge from storm or gale. Embraced by the welcoming arms of the two great piers, he was home, safe from the perils of the deep.

A. Duncan, Gravesend

The Lord Citrine, *the ship which carried the last cargo of coal from the Tyne in March 1998.*

The Dagenham, *owned by the Hudson Steam Ship Company, is seen as she blows her steam whistle while approaching the Tyne's Swing Bridge on August 31 1946. The* Dagenham *was one of the first ships to load at the electrically-operated Howdon Staith, opened in December 1932.*

Roker, Whitby, Flamborough, Spurn,
Outer Dowsing next on turn,
East Dudgeon and the Cromer bold
Look out for Haisborough and the Wold,
Then Kentish Knock, the Goodwins three
North, East and South in turn you'll see.

BIBLIOGRAPHY

Appleyard H.S. *The Constantine Group* (Kendal, 1983).

Carter J.M.C. *Stephenson Clarke* (Kendal, 1981).

Chesterton D. & Fenton R.S. *Gas and Electricity Colliers* (Kendal, 1984).

Foynes J.P. *The Battle of the East Coast* (1939-1945).

Garrett K.S. *Comben Longstaff & Co Ltd* (Gravesend, 1996).

Halpern P.G. *A Naval History of World War I* (London, 1994).

Keys R.E. *Dictionary of Tyne Sailing Ships* (Newcastle upon Tyne, 1998)

Larn R. & B. *Shipwreck Index of the British Isles* Vols 1-3 (London, 1996-98).

Lloyd's of London *Lloyd's War Losses – The First World War* (London, 1990).

Lloyd's of London *Lloyd's War Losses – The Second World War* (London, 1989).

MacRae J.A. & Waine C.V. *The Steam Collier Fleets* (Wolverhampton, 1990).

H.M.S.O. *O.H.M.S. British Coasters 1939-1945* (London, 1947).

River Tyne Official Handbook, 1925 & 1934 editions.

Newspapers, periodicals and magazines:
Lloyd's List, Newcastle Courant, Newcastle Journal, The Times, Nautical Magazine, Sea Breezes, Shipbuilding & Shipping Record.

Unpublished Ms:
Balmer B., transcriber. Matthew Jacobson, author. *Events in the Forty Two and a Half Years Seafaring Life of Matthew Jacobson, North Shields.*

INDEX TO VESSELS MENTIONED IN THE TEXT